# My Summer in Caillebotte's Garden

"The Painter under
His Parasol"
*1878.*
*Oil on canvas.*

## ACKNOWLEDGMENTS

The authors and publisher would like to thank:
M<sup>me</sup> Edith Acedo, M<sup>me</sup> Colette Argant, M. Jean-louis Daurelle and M<sup>me</sup> Marie-Jeanne Daurelle, M. Jean Gautier, president of the Société d'art, histoire et archéologie de la Vallée de l'Yerres, M. Gilbert Gobrecht, M<sup>me</sup> Françoise Lebiez, director of the Bibliothèque municipale de Brunoy, M<sup>me</sup> Pauline Paquin, M. Robert Schmit and Galerie Schmit, Galerie Brame and Lorenceau, M<sup>me</sup> Madeleine Vial.

We would also like to thank our advisory committee of young readers: Alice Dannaud, Aude and Cyrille Gogny-Goubert, and Amaury Chardeau and Capucine Gaillard, Caillebotte's two youngest descendants.

## PHOTO CREDITS

The color illustrations are taken from Pierre Wittmer, *Caillebotte and his Garden at Yerres* (New York, 1991), including: *The Nap*, p. 59, a work belonging to the Wadsworth Atheneum, Hartford, Connecticut (gift of the Wildenstein Foundation); *The Orange Trees*, p. 79, belonging to The Museum of Fine Arts, Houston (John A. and Audrey Jones Beck Collection); and *Bathers*, p. 67, Giraudon. The vignettes on pp. 14, 22, 23, 24, 38, 39, 40, 41, 46, 47, 48, 50, 54, 55, 60, 64, 65, and 80 are from the *Larousse agricole*, 1921 edition.

## THE DRAWINGS ARE BY:

Marie Hélène Chevalier, Pierre Henri Chevalier, Christine Dalisson, Claire Dannaud. The outline illustrations for coloring were traced from reproductions of drawings by Kate Greenaway (1846–1901), a British artist who was a contemporary of Caillebotte's.

Translated by
John Goodman

Word game by
Bryan Miller

Designed by Monelle Hayot
Typeset by Stéphanie Grenier
Color separations and printed by Mandarin Offset Ltd, Hong Kong

Front cover: *The Gardeners* (detail), 1875/77. Oil on canvas.

French editions: Monelle Hayot: ISBN 2-903824-19-3 and Réunion des musées nationaux, Paris: ISBN 2-7118-3130-2, under the title *Mon été avec Caillebotte*.

# Invitation to the Garden

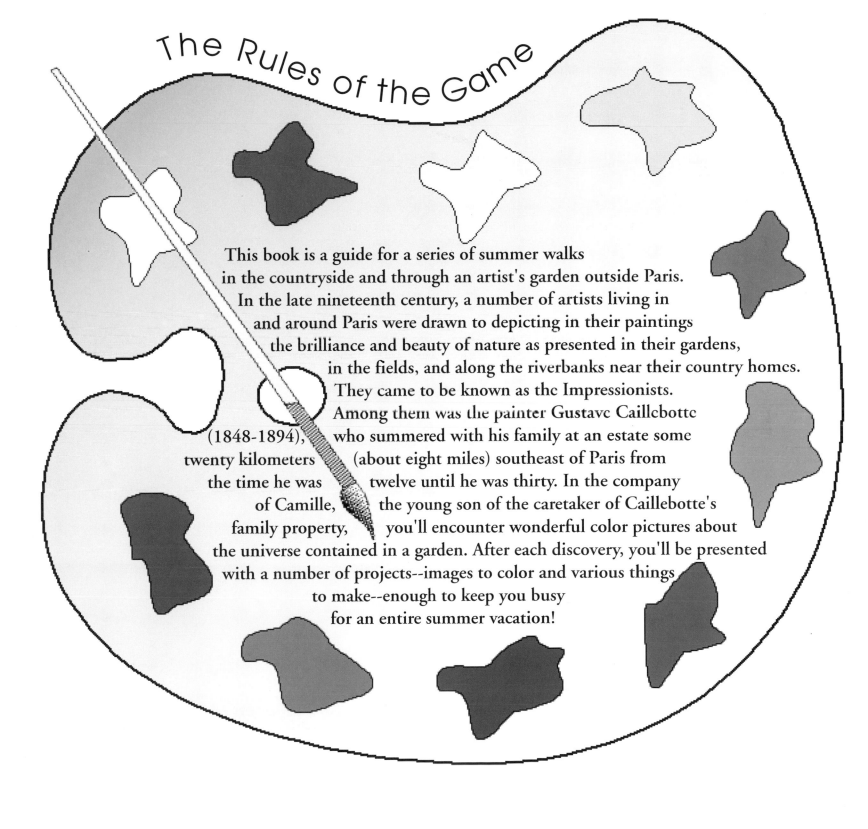

## The Rules of the Game

This book is a guide for a series of summer walks
in the countryside and through an artist's garden outside Paris.
In the late nineteenth century, a number of artists living in
and around Paris were drawn to depicting in their paintings
the brilliance and beauty of nature as presented in their gardens,
in the fields, and along the riverbanks near their country homes.
They came to be known as the Impressionists.
Among them was the painter Gustave Caillebotte
(1848-1894), who summered with his family at an estate some
twenty kilometers (about eight miles) southeast of Paris from
the time he was twelve until he was thirty. In the company
of Camille, the young son of the caretaker of Caillebotte's
family property, you'll encounter wonderful color pictures about
the universe contained in a garden. After each discovery, you'll be presented
with a number of projects--images to color and various things
to make--enough to keep you busy
for an entire summer vacation!

# To help you, here's
# A Calendar of Work in the Garden

*July*

In France school closes for summer vacation at the end of June. At the beginning of your vacation, plant some flower seeds (nasturtiums and baby's-breath), and you'll have flowers before the end of the summer—look at page 38.

Plant some radish seeds. In only three weeks, you'll have some to eat.

If you don't want to wait, buy and plant some small flowering plants that are about to bloom. You'll have flowers all summer—look at page 39.

Buy and transplant some small lettuce and tomato plants.

Harvest some cherries, strawberries, currants, and raspberries—look at the recipes on pages 47, 48, and 50.

Gather some flower petals and small leaves, and dry them in a big book. You'll need them—look at page 31.

Date  *July*  ❀

## Garden Diary

Make note here of what you did, the date, and your feelings about it.

It's impossible to take a vacation in the country and not become a gardener.
Try it, and you'll soon become fascinated!

Date  *August*  ❀

*August*

Pick some wildflowers and dry them—see page 54.

Harvest the radishes you planted in July.

Gather the lettuce you transplanted, now ready to eat.

Pick some peaches and plums from the orchard—see page 47.

Make some geranium cuttings—look at page 42.

Repot some impatiens.

And every day it's dry, be sure to water, cut off flowers that have faded, and loosen the ground around the flower plants: this makes it easier for air and water to reach the roots.

Hello. My name is Camille, I'm eight years old. My father is in charge of the Caillebotte family property at Yerres, which is in the country not too far from Paris. I live here, and I know this garden well. If you like, I'll be happy to act as your guide as we walk through it.

## From One Garden to Another
## with Camille

It's summer.

The picture on the following page, *The Park on the Caillebotte Property at Yerres*, reminds me of the sunny afternoons I've spent in this garden.

See the little girl walking along the path toward the bench? That's Zoé. She's dressed in clothes from 1875, when her cousin, the artist Gustave Caillebotte, painted this picture.

She's with a man I can't recognize from the back; he's wearing a summer suit and a straw hat to protect him from the sun. It might be one of her cousins, René or Martial, unless it's her uncle, who owns the beautiful white house whose columns and chimneys are visible in the background, beyond the lawn. It's an Italian-style manor.

Zoé comes here every summer, and spends a lot of time on the grounds, which are like a landscaped park. The gardeners have arranged big, bulging flower beds that resemble molehills. In the late spring, they plant geraniums in them that they potted and moved into the greenhouse around November 1, to shield them from the cold. When the flower beds are protected by shade, the gardeners plant them with impatiens.

Let's explore the park a bit. I'll show you some of its more interesting corners, where we'll play.

Here Zoé has just made her way through the little rose garden, which contains nothing but roses. Sometimes we call it the "school of roses"; some of the older varieties have funny names: "Nymph's Thigh," "Royal Purple," "Sultana," and "Snowball."

Overleaf:
"The Park
on the Caillebotte
Property at Yerres"
*1875.*
*Oil on canvas.*

# Learn to Predict the Weather

In the country, what you do on any given day is partly determined by whether it's raining or sunny.

The direction in which the wind blows can help you to predict the weather. Where I live, wind from the north usually brings cold air; it will be less warm.

Wind from the east usually means heat and dry weather; you'll have to do some watering.

Wind from the south usually means intense summer heat.

Wind from the west usually brings rain and wind. You should tie plants with long stems—dahlias for instance—to stakes in the ground.

*Morning sky*
"Sky Study, Clouds, Number 3"
*1872/78. Oil on canvas.*

*Evening sky*
"Sky Study, Clouds, Number 2"
*1872/78. Oil on canvas.*

## How?

By looking carefully at the sky.

If it's red early in the morning, some rain is likely to fall before noon. This is an excellent time to plant, because showers are good for newly planted seeds.

If it's pink at sunset, there will probably be wind the next day.

If the fruit in the orchard is ripe, try and pick it before nightfall.

# Gardening Tools

*String* *Rake* *Soil beater*

*For Planting*

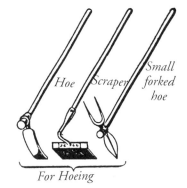

*Hoe* *Scraper* *Small forked hoe*

*For Hoeing*

you will use:

Spades allow you to turn the earth before sowing or planting. Small spades are handy for loosening the soil around flower beds or potted plants, and for removing weeds.

To sow straight, use a cord or string. Put a stake wound with string in the ground, unwind the string, stretch and tie it to the other stake, and make your furrow along the line it traces.

Wheelbarrows are useful in the garden to move all sorts of things: your tools, dead flowers that you've cut off, soil, etc.

Shovels and trowels are used to plant small plants and vegetables.

Pruning-shears are used constantly in the garden, for example to cut roses for the house and to cut off dead flowers and branches.

Rakes come in handy, too; there's nothing like a garden with well-raked paths.

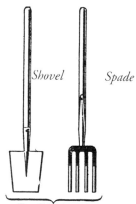

*Shovel* *Spade*

*For Digging*

# "Let's Go into the Woods"

It's very hot this afternoon.

At Yerres let's follow a path in the park that leads through some trees. It's shady and cool. We've left the sunny house, and right in the garden—what a surprise!— we find ourselves in the woods.

The landscape is bathed in golden sunlight that's pierced through the leaves of the trees. The sun makes big spots of light on the path in the foreground and illuminates the lawn in the background, beyond the tree trunks. The new grass will get scorched.

Caillebotte's name appears in the lower left of this painting. To create a gay effect, he used warm colors like red, yellow, and brown.

The cool colors are blue, green, and various grays.

But this landscape is especially warm, because it's painted mostly with yellows, along with light and dark browns.

The only cool parts are the small patches of blue sky visible through the leaves.

"Path Through
the Old-Growth
Woods
in the Park"
*1872/78.*
*Oil on canvas.*

It's decided : I want to make

# A Miniature Shade Garden!

The fancy name for this miniature shade garden is *terrarium*.

I am going to go into the woods to look for small mosses, lichens, young ferns, ivy, and other small plants that like shade and humidity.

I am bringing along some small bags, so that when I carefully dig up the plants I can keep enough dirt to cover their roots so they won't get hurt during the trip.

Back at the house, I find a jar, an old aquarium, or another kind of glass container.

On the bottom, I place a layer of sand about an inch deep, and then a thick layer of soil from the garden.

Then I plant my lichens, ferns, and other marvelous gatherings in the soil; I water them lightly and cover the top with a piece of cardboard pierced with some air holes.

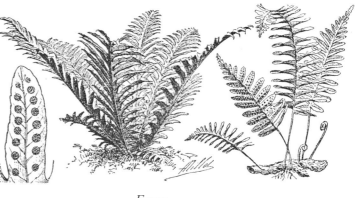

*Ferns*

I put my jar in a place far from daylight, protected from the sun.

And my shade garden will thrive like this, producing its own humidity.

I'll water it only rarely, but with my little scissors I'll make sure to cut off dry and broken leaves—and I'll look inside a lot!

*Lichens*

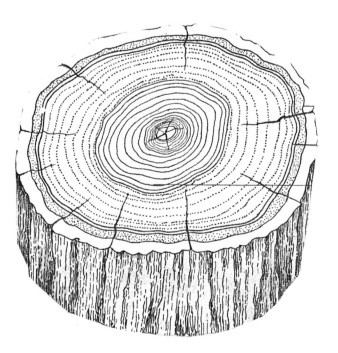

*Each ring represents one year.*
*Narrow rings indicate dry years.*
*When all the rings are thicker on one side,*
*that's where the tree was exposed to the most light.*

## How Old is This Tree?

If you come across a tree trunk in the woods, look carefully at its concentric rings.

Each ring or circle corresponds to a year in the tree's life. You can determine its age by counting the rings.

Each ring represents another year's growth. The rings also indicate which years were dry, for when they're thin that means the tree didn't grow very much. They also tell us which way the tree faced; on the north side, they will be narrower than on the south, which receives more light. This effect tends to make the circles into ovals.

If you get lost in the woods, look carefully at the trunks of the trees: the bark on their northwest sides is mossy.

## "Do You Prefer His Hat or Mine?"

In the distance, I see someone sitting on a stone bench and wearing a Panama hat. I approach him quietly, without making a sound. It's Gustave Caillebotte, the painter.

On an easel in front of him are a mirror and a rectangular canvas. He's painting *Self-Portrait in a Summer Hat*. I think it's the first time he's painted himself in the garden.

I can still remember him painting this picture with broad brush strokes, especially for the tree trunks on the right. He certainly got his own face right; it's as though I were still looking at him.

I was still little at the time. I thought he was playing with colors: I didn't dare disturb him, so I hid behind a tree and watched.

In those years, I was fascinated by the many different kinds of tree bark.

"Self-Portrait in a Summer Hat"
*1872/78.*
*Oil on canvas.*

*Pine*

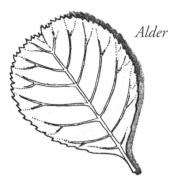

*Alder*

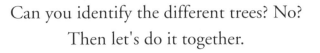

Can you identify the different trees? No?
Then let's do it together.

*Planer tree*

*Yew*

Let's go into the woods on a dry, sunny day to watch the light play over the leaves of the trees, and to collect two leaf samples of each of the species we recognize.

We'll take a small drawing pad with sheets of newspaper inside folded in half; we'll carefully place the leaves we collect in the newspaper, where they'll be safe until we get home.

Then we'll dry one leaf of each species.

We'll wait a week or so—no less!—and then check to see if our leaves are really dry. In the meantime, we'll look up the names of the rest of the leaves using these eighteen illustrations of some of the more common trees. We'll write down the names of those we've matched. We may have collected a few that aren't pictured here. We can look those up in an illustrated dictionary or encyclopedia, paying close attention to their shapes. Such reference books exist for the trees of most every country in the world.

When the leaves are good and dry, we'll carefully place them on the pages of a notebook, using pincers if possible. Then we'll use transparent glue—not too much!—to attach them to the pages.

*Maple*

*Dogwood*

*Southern
White Cedar*

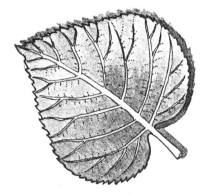

*Linden*

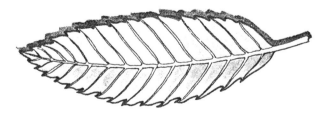

*Chestnut*

Judas tree

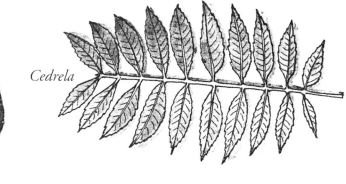
Cedrela

Gingko

## A Collection of Dried Leaves

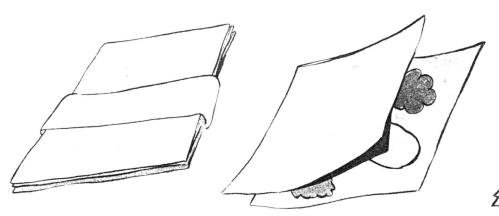

*Use blotting-paper capable of absorbing the leaves' humidity.*

*Carefully place the leaves between two sheets, perfectly flat.*

*Place the sheets of paper inside a newspaper, and then put a big book on top of it.*

*Ash*

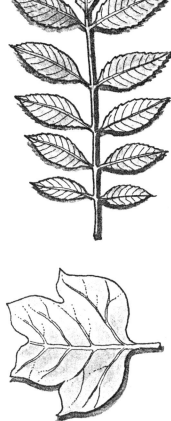

On a sheet of drawing-paper, we'll write the name of each species of tree, as well as the date when and place where we gathered it. No mistakes!

And we'll have made a notebook of dried foliage samples. If you like, we could make a similar book of dried flowers.

*Cedar*

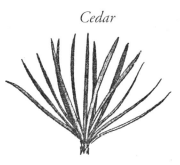

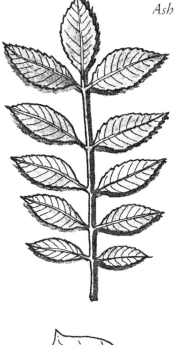
*Tulip tree*

*Poplar*

*Chestnut*

# "Here I Am at the Foot of an Oak"

How well I remember! My father worked through the hot months at Yerres, in the country house of Monsieur and Madame Martial Caillebotte, where the whole family spent the summer.

There were four sons: Gustave (the painter), his brothers René and Martial, and his half-brother Alfred. And then there was their cousin Zoé, whom we've already met.

The painter liked to use me as a model because I didn't move. When you're being painted, you need to keep still for long periods of time.

On this particular day, he found me sitting at the foot of an oak tree in the wooded area, where I was trying to listen to the birds.

*Oak*

"Camille Daurelle under an Oak Tree" *1872/78. Oil on cardboard.*

20

G. Caillebotte

# I Want to Learn How to Recognize the Birds in My Garden

Sit down in some thick bushes or at the foot of a tree, like Camille; then get comfortable and remain still. After a few minutes, you will be rewarded: you'll see and hear a great many different birds. There are hundreds of species of birds in France, but don't worry; I'm only going to identify eight of them here! Some might stay in your garden all summer, but others will only pay brief visits.

Let's start with the ones that are easiest to recognize:

### The Magpie

Its long tail and black-and-white plumage make it easy to spot; it's afraid of nothing and comes right up to the house, making lots of noise! Perhaps you already know that it's attracted to anything that glitters: it's the "thieving magpie" that brings "jewels" back to its nest. Take a good look at its white belly and the small, white splotches on each of its wings.

### The Blackbird

You can't miss this one: it's black all over. The only notes of color are its bright yellow beak and the small yellow circles around its eyes. It can often be seen hopping over the lawn looking for worms. What it loves most is fruit from the orchard: if you don't pick it first, you're out of luck! Its song is one of the most beautiful you'll hear in the garden.

*If you have binoculars, they're perfect for birdwatching!*

*Magpie*

*Blackbird*

### The Great Tit

It has a yellow belly, its back has a greenish cast, and its head features white cheeks and a shiny black skull-cap. It's not rare, and it loves to hang upside-down from branches.

### The Song Thrush

What a pretty name! Its white-spotted belly stands out, but the plumage on its back is a uniform brown.

### Robin Redbreast

Like the tit, it will gladly set up house in a nesting place you've prepared for it. Take a flowerpot, widen the hole in the bottom (this will be the entrance), and attach it to a tree with some sturdy wire. With a little help, you can also hammer a few boards together and attach them to a tree trunk.

The redbreast not only has a bright red-orange breast—hence its name—but also a throat of the same color. The khaki-maroon plumage on its back and wings harmonizes perfectly with its red feathers.

### The Green Woodpecker

The way it clambers up tree trunks makes it easy to spot. It grips the bark with its hooked feet and uses its sharp beak to poke holes as it looks for insects; it's especially fond of ants. Its plumage is pale green, becoming almost yellow toward the tail, and its head is red with white cheeks.

*Song Thrush*

*Robin Redbreast*

*Green Woodpecker*

Green Woodpecker

*Swallow*

## The Swallow

If you live in the north of France, this bird is in your garden only during the summer; it arrives late in the spring and heads south again at the first sign of frost. You've probably already noticed its long, forked tail and pointed wings. The feathers on its back are a glossy black; its throat and chest are black, too, but they aren't so shiny. Its cup-shaped nests are made of earth and straw, and are sometimes found attached to the beams or rafters in a barn; it returns to the same nest every spring, repairing it when necessary.

## The Turtle Dove

There's no confusing the turtle dove with the common pigeon, even though they both coo languorously: this one is much more elegant and has ash-gray feathers.

*Turtle Dove*

Turtle Dove

*Artificial nests*

If you ferret through the woods and look under trees and in the underbrush, you're very likely to find bird feathers.

Why not arrange and glue them onto the pictures of the birds you recognize?

You can finish their plumage with touches of watercolor or crayon. You could make the birds look like they're about to fly away!

Blackbird

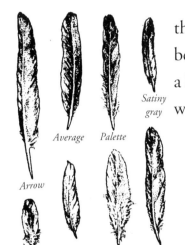

*Arrow*    *Average*    *Palette*    *Satiny gray*

*Small eyelet*    *Satiny white*    *Swimmer*    *Ashen*

But before gluing down your feathers, be sure to dry them in the same way you dried the leaves, placing them flat between two sheets of blotting paper and covering them with a heavy book for several days. If they aren't completely dry, they won't last as long.

Magpie

*Palette*  *Knife*  *Arrows*  *Average*  *Shell*

*Small down*

*Marabou
or
large down*

Tit

Song Thrush

Caricature of
a Gardener and
a Pumpkin,
c. *1876.*
*Pencil.*

## "Let's Look for the Gardener"

Sometimes I want to get as far away as I can from the white summer house with its columns.

After passing through the wooded glade, I run to a little blue door leading to the kitchen garden. There I'm sure to find the gardener or one of his four assistants.

On this particular day, I surprised him as he was bending over the lawn next to the flower beds, pulling weeds. He always kept some pruning-shears in the pocket of his blue apron.

It's interesting to talk to gardeners, because they always answer the questions you ask them. Sometimes they even explain what they're doing.

That's how I picked up a thing or two about gardening. I learned to recognize the tools, and now I even know what each one is used for.

The gardener explained to me that these flower beds were reserved for cutting flowers, used to make the magnificent bouquets for rooms in the house.

The walls of the kitchen garden are covered with trellises, along which climb sweet peas. I love the colors of their flowers: there are so many! And they smell so nice!

"The Gardener"
*1877. Oil on canvas.*

*The ladybug's convex wing-sheaths spread apart when it wishes to fly.*

Heads-up! listen to

## The Story of the Ladybug!

This little insect is a great friend of gardeners. And since you're becoming one yourself. . .

It's easy to recognize this tiny creature. The best-known ladybug is red with seven black spots, but there are others that are yellow or orange-black, with two spots, or even as many as twenty!

But why is the ladybug so popular with gardeners?

Because it's the hungriest animal you'll ever see. It devours aphids, which infest the leaves, branches, and buds of plants—roses for instance—sucking up their sap. A single ladybug can eat a hundred aphids each day, and the larvae eat as many as a hundred and fifty! When ladybugs are cleaning a rosebud that's infested with aphids, it's something to see: they act just like an insecticide, but they're preferable because they're not toxic. Large numbers of ladybugs are even grown in laboratories and then released into cultivated fields.

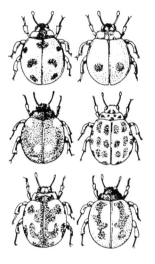

## How Good the Garden Smells!

Is there some way to bring this delicious odor into the house and keep it there?

Yes, by making potpourri.

This eighteenth-century French term designates a pot of aromatic foliage intended to perfume a room.

Rose petals are an essential element of these preparations, which also include spices, peels, perfumed woods, aromatic plants, and essential oils.

Here's a very simple recipe for

## A Real Rose Potpourri

Gather and dry three large handfuls of rose petals and rosebuds. When they're dry, place them in a pretty bowl. Add two tablespoons of powdered cinnamon, half a tablespoon of cloves, a small vanilla bean, and five drops of essence of rose (see page 32). Then gently mix everything together. A marvelous odor will emanate from the bowl for several months, perfuming the entire room.

*You can also add dried geranium petals.*

# Roses

"Let's pick, let's pick roses in the morning of our lives."

LAMARTINE

Yes, pick roses in the garden to decorate and scent the house—or paint them like Caillebotte did!

Is there anything else we might we do? Why not make rosewater? I'll tell you how rosewater was invented. In the tenth century, an Eastern princess prepared for an elaborate party by throwing a large number of rose petals into the canal surrounding her residence. The sun was so hot that it distilled the rose petals, and what we call essence of rose, or rosewater, appeared on the surface of the water. It was collected and preserved in bottles.

Here's how you can make your own rosewater. It's easy! Pick six beautiful perfumed roses, remove their petals, and boil them for a half hour in a pint and a half of mineral water.

Add a small carrot that's been cut in half to soften the water. Then filter everything through a strainer, pour the liquid into a pretty bottle or vial, and let it cool.

*Rosewater is a wonderful toilet water*
*for softening the skin!*

"Garden Rose and Blue Forget-Me-Nots in a Vase"
*1872/78.*
*Oil on canvas.*

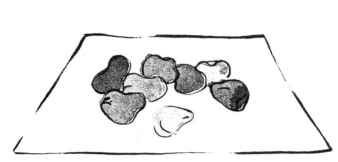

Another idea!

## Sachets of Rose Petals

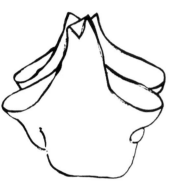

Rose-petal sachets have long been used to perfume linen and clothing. They're placed between the folded linen in closets and in drawers. Some people even hang them up—a lovely thing to do!

First, dry some perfumed rose petals in the shade by spreading them out flat on a dishcloth in a well-ventilated place.

After they're dry, tear them into little pieces and place them in a salad bowl. Then add some cloves and a bit of grated nutmeg (there's probably some in your kitchen).

1. Lay out some small squares of fabric. Place a handful of your mixture on each one.

2. Bring together the four corners of each square.

3. Tie each square securely with some strong string, and you're done! Don't hesitate to make several at a time.

If you sew:

You can use the same mixture to make a small, square cushion.

*Add a ribbon
and tie a pretty knot.*

Cut two pieces of fabric about six inches square, sew them together along three sides, fill the pad with your mixture, and then sew together the fourth side.

*Choose a material you like,
cotton if possible. You can add
a lace border and embroider
a rose in the middle.*

# For Those Who Like to Eat, Rose Honey

A recipe that's quite refined but easy to make!

First collect about half a pound of strongly perfumed rose petals (weigh them on a scale). Place them in a salad bowl and add a little less than a pint of boiling water. Stir gently and then leave undisturbed for twenty-four hours. The next day, strain the liquid and then pour it into a cooking pot and add about two pounds of honey. Heat gently until the mixture becomes a very thick syrup. Stir well, remove from the heat, and pour the syrup into small jars you've prepared in advance. The result is delicious!

All that's left for you to do is cut out little labels and write "Rose Honey," the date, and "Made by: . . . . . . " (your name) on them. Then glue them on.

Maybe you'll want to draw a little rose on each label, too.

*Beehives in a stand*

# "Do You Want to Come with Me to the Kitchen Garden?"

On another walk, I go even farther. I cross the flower garden to see if there's any ripe fruit in the kitchen garden, which is also a fruit garden. These utility gardens make it possible for us to have fresh fruit and vegetables all summer long without going to the market.

The plan of this garden is simple and straightforward; it was designed for easy maintenance. In the center, where two perpendicular paths cross, there's a basin of water that can be used to water the plants. The rest of the space is divided into plots in which herbs and vegetables are arranged in successive rows, making a checkerboard of different plant beds. This garden, like the flower garden, is surrounded by a wall to protect the plants from the wind and to help retain the heat from the sun, which makes fruit ripen faster, and vegetables reach maturity earlier.

The painter placed his easel on the garden's axis, in order to give his composition a symmetrical, geometric character.

"The Kitchen Garden, Yerres" *1875/77. Oil on canvas.*

# Gardening

*Radish*

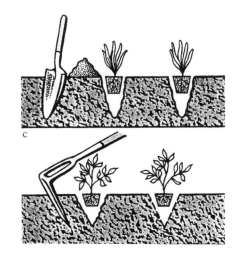

*Planting*

Today I sow and plant.

I have at my disposal a small corner of the garden that's rather sunny. I begin by preparing the soil; if it hasn't been "worked" in a long time, I turn over the soil with a spade, breaking it up to aerate it and make it easier to remove any weeds. Then I rake it smooth again. Finally everything is ready for sowing. I begin by sowing radishes: I stretch out my string and drop seeds from the packet along its length. I cover the seeds with a thin layer of soil, I water them a bit, and then I wait. Three or four weeks later, there will be radishes for me to harvest—if I don't forget to water them, that is.

I can also sow love-in-a-mist, which will quickly produce a beautiful blue flower surrounded by a light collarette; or nasturtiums, which produce little round leaves after a few days, and in a month or so orange and red flowers. If you don't have access to a real bit of garden, you can plant the seeds in large pots that are placed in the sun.

*Parsely, which you can plant, too*

*Sowing*

*Anthemums*

*Nasturtiums*

*Petunias*

Sometimes I don't want to wait.

Then I buy plants that are already grown from seeds. They have stems, leaves, and sometimes even flower buds that are about to open. These plants are sold in little plastic pots. After we buy them, it's up to me to replant them, either in my corner of the garden or in a big flower pot.

With a shovel or a planting scoop, I dig a hole the right size, and then I carefully remove the little plastic pot from the clod of soil. Little roots run all through it. I loosen it a bit, very delicately, with my fingers; then I place it in the hole, pack down the soil (not too hard!), and water it. This little plant will grow and bloom all summer; there's a big selection of plants I can buy: geraniums, verbena, petunias, anthemums, impatiens, and marigolds, as well as lettuce and tomato plants that will continue to grow until we eat their produce at the end of the summer.

*Geraniums*

*Verbena*

*Lettuce*

*Tomato plants*

*Field mice*

# Do Gardeners Regard These Animals as Friends or Enemies?

*Hedgehog*

You may be familiar with the hedgehog, the little mammal that can easily be tamed. Place some bread and milk in a corner of the garden every day, and it's very likely you'll soon see one. The hedgehog comes out at night, after it's dark, for that's when it hunts the snails, slugs, and insects that it usually eats.

Is the hedgehog a friend or an enemy? (Cross out the wrong answer.)

It's much more difficult to get a look at a mole! Its long front feet, which are extremely powerful, are used to dig underground passages in which it feeds on earthworms. Molehills—the little piles of soil you sometimes see on lawns—are made from earth that it's excavated during the digging of these passages.

Is the mole a friend or an enemy?

The field mouse resembles the ordinary mouse, but if you look closely you'll see that its tail is thinner and its ears are larger. It is also a warmer tone of brown and its belly is touched with white. This little rodent feeds on peas, fruit, seeds, and bulbs in the garden.

Is the field mouse a friend or an enemy?

*Mole*

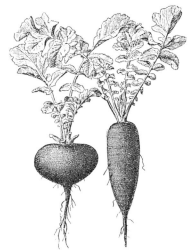

*Round and oblong radishes*

What can I do today?
I know!

## A Root Garden

*Different kinds of carrot*

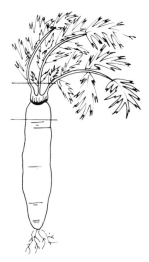

We've brought back from the kitchen garden or the market some root vegetables like radishes, carrots, turnips, and celery.

I begin by filling a bowl with little stones and water. I can choose pretty ones.

Then I cut the vegetables, leaving half an inch of the root and about the same amount of foliage. Then I place these little "stumps" in my bowl.

I place the bowl in the sun, on a windowsill or on a small table in the garden, and a few days later new leaves will appear, giving me a little portable garden.

The leaves will grow; the roots will not.

But the resulting greenery is pretty, so I'll enjoy it for a while.

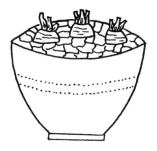

Today

# I Take Some Cuttings
## and Do Some Transplanting

My geranium is very beautiful. I can make three or four more from the same plant. How?

By taking cuttings.

What is a cutting? It's a small branch of a plant that you cut off and put in a pot; you take it from the upper portion of the "mother plant," in this case my beautiful geranium. It should be between three and four inches long and have about six leaves but no flowers or buds, and it should always be severed just above a leaf. Then you plant it in a large pot of soil and water it immediately. Soon it will grow its own roots and have its own flowers. The pot should be kept in a cool and damp place away from sun and wind.

There's some beautiful impatiens in my garden. I'd like to keep it inside over the winter, so I decide to take it out of the garden and transplant it into a pot I can move into the house. I choose a big pot and place some rocks over the hole in the bottom; this keeps in the soil but lets excess liquid pass through when I water. Then I put some good soil in. Now I'm ready to dig up my impatiens and transplant it into the pot.

## "Is This the Right Time to Water the Green Beans?"

When I visit the kitchen garden on very hot summer days, usually in the late afternoon, I always find the gardeners in their blue aprons doing their watering. It's a feast for the eyes—just like in the painting on the next page, which shows two barefoot gardeners in blue aprons watering the green beans. The little glass market-garden cloches behind them, lifted slightly on clay pots so the plants underneath can breathe, seem like hats about to dance.

In the background are hotbeds for the forced growth of young plants in compost soil. Their glazed tops are lifted a bit so the plants won't suffocate for lack of air and too much heat, for the sun really beats down in late morning and early afternoon. If it gets cooler as evening approaches, the tops can be closed. In some of the hotbeds, the plants are in small, clay pots set into the compost, while in others they're planted directly in the ground. Sometimes I help the gardener pull up radishes: he shakes off the soil, rinses them off, and ties them into bunches.

The long wall hit by the sun on the right is planted with peach trees. When I place my hands on the wall, I can feel the heat of the stone. I keep close tabs on the peaches; I love to watch them ripen, and sometimes they turn red in the course of a single day. You have to be careful of the wasps attracted by the fruit. The opposite wall is planted with pear trees; they are espaliered over the wall's surface on wooden trellises.

Behind the wall, you can see a row of poplars in the adjacent field that blocks the north wind.

Overleaf:
"The Gardeners"
*1875/77.*
*Oil on canvas.*

# Learning to Water

Watering is necessary to make seeds sprout, flowering plants bloom, and vegetables grow.

Plants can die if they don't get enough water.

First of all, look at the soil. If it's cold and damp, it doesn't need water. If it's dry and powdery, then water it. Don't ever do this in direct sunlight; early morning and late afternoon are the best times. In the summer, the twilight hours are preferable; less moisture will evaporate then, and all the water will reach the roots. And they need a lot of it after a hot day.

It's best to water some plants, like roses and plants in window boxes, without wetting their leaves and flowers, which means delivering the water directly to their roots. To do that, you can use the upper portion of a plastic bottle as a kind of gullet; push it into the soil and pour in the water. The liquid will reach the roots without getting the flowers wet.

## The Fruit in Your Garden, or Your Neighbor's

July and August are the months for harvesting peaches, plums, strawberries, and currants.

So gather them and eat your fill along the way—but don't make yourself sick!

Bring home what's left and make the recipes on the following pages. Your family and friends will be able to eat some of them the same day; others will produce fruit preserves, making it possible to taste a bit of summer when it's nothing but a memory.

## Strawberry Soup

### original and delicious

Gather enough very ripe strawberries to fill a large salad bowl. Wash them gently and remove their stems. Cut them in half and place them in a big pot. Add about half a pound of sugar and enough water to cover everything. Heat gently, watching closely while stirring constantly with a wooden spoon, to make sure the fruit doesn't stick to the bottom. Take some thick bread and cut it into small cubes; place these in soup bowls and pour the strawberry soup over them.

Now it's time to call your friends. And tell them to hurry— strawberry soup is best when it's warm.

# Peach Charlotte

*a simple recipe*

- some ripe peaches
- a small container of heavy whipping cream
- some powdered sugar
- two boxes of finger biscuits
- a deep mold

Wash and peel the fruit, cut it into pieces, and place the pieces in a bowl with a little sugar.

Line the bottom and sides of the mold with the finger biscuits. Whip the cream until thick, but do not overwhip.

Place a layer of the peaches in the mold, then a layer of whipped cream, then some sugar, then another layer of peaches, another of whipped cream, and more sugar, etc., until the mold is completely filled. Place it in the refrigerator with a plate on top, let it sit for three hours, and then enjoy!

## Colored Fruit

I remember the scene very well. Some fruit from the garden had been arranged on a table in a room close to the kitchen. The painter had set up his easel and placed a small rectangular canvas on it. When I asked him what he was painting, he said it was a "still life." I wanted those pieces of fruit. It was only after he'd finished his canvas that he permitted us—Zoé and myself—to take them. We were both wearing aprons, and it's a good thing, too: those pieces of fruit were full of juice, and we made a mess eating them.

The still life looks great. I'd eat those peaches, nectarines, and apricots all over again.

"Peaches,
Nectarines, and
Apricots"
*1872/78.*
*Oil on canvas*

49

# Red-Currant Jelly

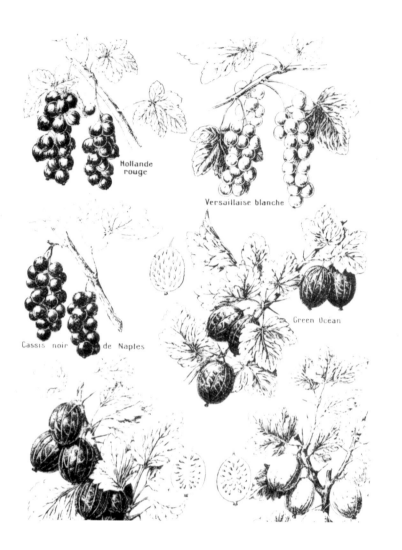

*Photograph a jar of your jelly
and paste it here!*

Absolutely delicious—and fast, too!

You'll need about two pounds of red currants. Wash them, let them drip dry, and then crush them in a vegetable mill.

Take the beautiful juice that you get and set it aside for an hour. Then weigh it and put it into a large container along with its weight in powdered sugar. Mix everything together with a wooden spoon until the sugar has completely melted; then pour the mixture into jars. The jelly will thicken in a day or two, and meantime you can glue labels to the jars. Then it's ready to eat. But don't wait too long: nothing in it has been cooked, so it won't last beyond the end of the summer.

# A Magic Pear

When pears first appear, in July, they're very small. Before they've gotten too big, place one that is still on the tree in an empty clear-glass bottle with a wide neck. Then attach the bottle to the tree, being careful not to break the fruit's stem.

This pear will grow faster than the others, because the bottle protects the fruit and concentrates the sunlight and the warmth.

When the pear fills the bottle, cut the stem, take the bottle down from the tree, and fill it with liquor such as brandy. Add about 3-1/2 ounces of sugar and close tightly.

The bottle should sit in the sun for a few days before its contents are tasted. Since, of course, liquor is not for children, this will make a lovely gift for your parents, or adults friends and relatives.

And don't forget to ask people to guess how you were able to get such a big pear into the bottle!

## "But Where Did the Cows Go?"

It's always a pleasure to walk through the fields speckled with flowers.

After running through the landscaped park, I come to a small stone bridge over the canal that brings water to the kitchen garden.

I stop, out of breath, and look at the surface of the water, which reflects the sky. I throw a rock into the slumbering water and then continue across the bridge. Then I'm in a big field. The grasses are very high, for they haven't been mown. A row of poplars reminds me of motionless lead soldiers in formation.

At the far edge of the field, I see a woman seated under a tree. She's grazing her cow. I like to visit with her, for she knows the strange names of all the wild plants. Some of them have spectacular flowers, which fill the field with colors: it's a veritable garden in which cows are welcome.

"Woman Seated
under a Tree"
*1872/73.*
*Oil on canvas.*

# Let's Learn about Wildflowers

*Corn-poppy*

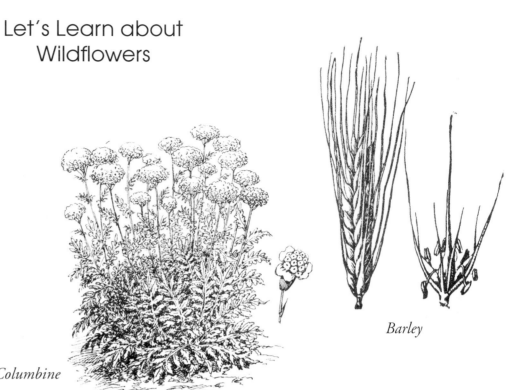

*Columbine*

*Barley*

*Wheat*

The flowers that grow in meadows, along roads, and at the edge of fields are often just as beautiful as flowers cultivated in gardens. Let's learn to recognize a few of them.

You can pick some to make a big bouquet for the house, but be sure to cut the stems: if you pull up the roots, the flower won't be able to grow again next year.

*Clover*  *Marguerite*  *Knapweed*  *Oats*

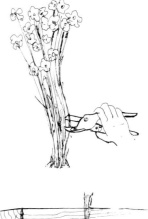

You can also pick some flowers and dry them to make a bouquet that will last all winter. You'll be able to find columbine growing by the side of the road in August. Cut the stems with some pruning shears, remove the lower leaves, tie them together near the ends with some string, and then hang them upside down. After a month or so, they'll be ready for you to arrange your bouquet. You can use any kind of flower. Don't forget to include some grassy plants such as oats, barley, and wheat in your arrangement; they'll give it a deliciously wild character.

*Valerian*

*Buttercup*

*Daisy*

In the meadow, I make

# daisy crowns

Pick some field daisies with long stems.

Weave them together, adding another flower whenever the stems cross over one another.

As you proceed, cut off any unnecessary branches and leaves.

When the string of flowers is long enough, weave in a few stems to add strength. Then weave the loose stems at the end into the point where you started, securing them as best you can.

While we've chosen here to work with daisies, you can make crowns or wreathes like this with any long-stemmed flower that appeals to you.

# Draw your bouquet
## of wildflowers

Use whatever you like: pastels, watercolor, colored crayons, or felt-tip pens.

# "The siesta is the best part of the day"

When it's hot, the meadow can be pleasantly cool. An impressive silence reigns there. I often explore it before the tall grasses are cut, to hide out and watch the bees and insects.

On this particular day, I headed across the garden to the other side of the road, where the meadow begins, and came upon a man napping on a blanket. He fascinated me. He was sleeping deeply. I never found out who he was or if I knew him, for he had placed his Panama hat over his face to protect it from bugs and the sun. It was as though he thought of the meadow as the Land of Cockaigne, the imaginary country where there's plenty of everything, so you can have whatever you want without difficulty, even if you spend most of your time just lying around.

What a stroke of luck that Gustave Caillebotte arrived at this moment with his pastels. He stopped a short distance away, signaled me not to make any noise, and quickly executed this picture of *The Nap*. I can still see him working on it.

"The Nap"
*1877.*
*Pastel.*

# Garden visitors

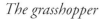

*The locust*

*The field cricket*

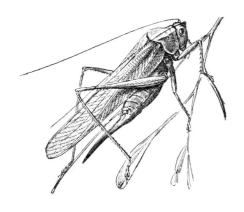

*The grasshopper*

If you want to see a few, sit down in the meadow and look for them in the high grasses. Maybe you'll be lucky enough to come across a grasshopper, a locust, or a cricket!

It's easy to tell them apart. The locust has shorter antennae than the grasshopper, and when it jumps it spreads its wings so it'll go farther. Look at the grasshopper's long back legs; they allow it to jump high. You might hear these insects before you see them, for both "sing" by rubbing their wing-sheaths together; if you want to use the correct word to describe this, say that they're "chirring."

The field cricket, which is a beautiful black and has glistening eyes, also chirrs, though it does so by rubbing its back legs against its wing-sheaths. It lives in a burrow it digs in loose soil and usually comes out only at night.

Would you like to learn how to make crickets come out of their burrows? First, figure out where the cricket's song is coming from and move toward the sound as quietly as possible. But note the position of the sun: if you throw a shadow on the cricket, it will stop singing immediately.

When you think you're getting close, crawl along the ground, trying not to disturb the earth. You can spot the burrow, which is shaped like a little tunnel. The cricket will probably be at the front of it. Gently insert a small stick in the burrow about two inches from the entrance, so the cricket can't retreat into its depths. It will surely come out, and then—finally!—you can see it! Take a good look, but then remove your stick and let the cricket return to its home.

## Story-time

Write a poem or tell a story

## "*Quiet, we're fishing!*"

I was forbidden to go by myself to the banks of the nearby river, called the Yerres. So every time I could go there in the company of a grown-up was a special event.

On this particular day, Zoé and I were playing in the garden when we saw a man with a fishing-rod pass by; after a while, we decided to go and see if he'd caught anything in the river. Zoé had her own fishing-rod; she got it and we approached without making any noise, walking on tiptoes. In Gustave Caillebotte's *Fishing*, the fisherman is seated, looking for any sign of movement beneath the water's surface. Everything is still and serene; he might have to wait a long time before he gets a nibble.

Caillebotte wasn't fishing; he was sitting close by at his easel and painting this picture. I was fascinated by his way of applying little dabs of paint to the canvas, like so many colored sparks of light.

"Fishing"
*1878.
Oil on canvas.*

Learn to recognize the kinds of fish you might be able to catch in a stream or river near the place where you vacation. In the Yerres River, these are some of the fish I caught:

Minnow: *A small fish about four inches long, very common in rivers and streams.*

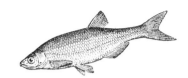

Bleak: *This European fish has silvery white sides and a dark green back; it's about six inches long and prefers slow-moving water.*

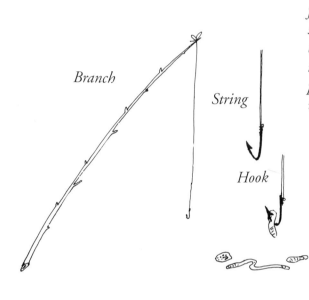

*Branch*

*String*

*Hook*

*Bait*

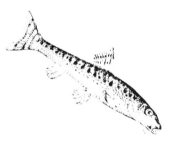

Roach: *It has an oval shape, large scales, and is 6 to 12 inches long. It can be caught with bits of bread.*

Gudgeon: *The marbled brown, black-spotted back of this fish makes it easy to recognize; it's about six inches long and is especially abundant in August and September.*

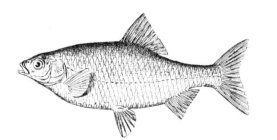

On the riverbank,

## I try my hand at fishing

Frogs: *To catch a frog, attach a bit of red cloth to your hook.*

I don't have a fishing-rod, but that's no problem.

You can make one from a flexible branch that's bent a bit; just attach to its end some string equipped with a hook.

You'll need some bait—a worm, an insect, or a bit of bread—for your hook (put it on carefully!). Then cast your line into the water and wait, without moving or talking.

When you feel a tug, pull the line out of the water, take the fish gently in your hands, carefully remove the hook, and try to recognize it quickly.

Then you have two options:

1) You throw it back into the water.

2) You place it in a box or a basket to take home and cook—but don't catch more fish than you can eat!


There are rules you must follow:

Don't run away from the riverbank without a thought, leaving trash there.

Don't stomp in the water to scare the fish.

And above all, be careful with the hooks.

## *"Into the water!"*

When the weather's nice in the country, it's fun to go swimming. Remember that you should never go swimming without someone else who is a good swimmer. Whoever is with you can help if you find yourself in trouble.

A century ago, swimming pools were rare. You had to learn to swim in rivers, streams, and lakes with clear, clean water.

Improvised diving boards were sometimes set up at places on the shore where people liked to bathe for fun.

It's very likely that the man in this painting seen climbing out of the water on the right has just dived; now it's his companion's turn. The diver is wearing a kind of bathing suit that was fashionable in the late nineteenth century.

Painters usually represent actions for which models can hold long poses without moving, in several sessions if necessary. But here Gustave Caillebotte caught the diver just as he is about to plunge into the water. It's a bit as though he had taken a photograph of this man.

The scene is made to appear quite gay by the striking use of blues and greens.

Lighter colors give the water a sense of transparency and make it seem to move before our eyes.

"Bathers"
*1878.*
*Oil on canvas.*

## Swimming in Caillebotte's time

In the years 1860-78, when Gustave Caillebotte spent his summer vacations at Yerres, swimming was an important leisure activity.

Because of its beneficial effects on the body, it was made a part of the normal educational process; it was also taught in military schools, for, besides strengthening the muscles, it increases stamina and improves coordination. It was relatively rare for women and girls to swim in public during this period, as it was for them to sail.

In those days, swimming lessons began on dry land. Students were instructed to lie on their bellies on special stools, stretch out, and practice the stroking and kicking motions.

Only later, after these swimming-in-the-air exercises, were they permitted to enter the water, usually a river. They were told to wade in until immersed up to the chest and turn around to face the shore. Then they were instructed to throw an egg into the clear water in front of them and dive in after it, keeping their eyes open and using the hand and feet motions they had learned.

After defeating their initial fear of the water in this way, they learned the breast stroke, which involves moving the arms and legs like a frog. Then they were taught to dive and

learned other strokes. (In Caillebotte's day, it was thought that, once the new swimmer was at ease in the water, his course of training should be completed by his learning to swim while clothed: after initial sessions in bathing trunks, the student was instructed to add shoes, pants, shirt, etc., until he could swim well fully dressed!) Here are some of the other strokes:

The crawl: Facing down but turning your head in the same direction periodically for air, move forward by extending first your right then your left arm over and then into the water with your fingers cupped, sweeping it back to your hip; repeat this double motion over and over, in coordination with steady, straight-legged kicks.

The dogpaddle: Keeping your head above the surface, make alternating up and down motions with your right and left hands and feet, like a dog in the water.

The sidestroke: Lying on your side, and keeping your limbs underwater or just below the surface at all times, move your lower arm above your head and your lower arm to your chest and back. As you do this, draw your legs up, bent at the knees, opening the top leg toward the front and the bottom toward the black before bringing them back together .

Treading water: stay afloat with your head above water and your body perpendicular to the surface by moving your legs and feet smoothly and constantly, stroking your hands gently just beneath the surface to keep yourself from tilting over.

What other strokes do you know?

# "Quick, it's going to rain"

When I was in the garden on this particular day, I was wondering what I should do. I was nervous, because it looked like it was going to rain.

I stayed close to the house. At precisely that moment, Gustave Caillebotte came outside with his box of pastels. He had seen me and asked me to remain still. He then made this picture very fast, though not fast enough to suit me. I'm seen in profile, silhouetted against a section of path; the flower beds behind me resemble two bouquets. The artist signed this work on the upper left with a "G," his first initial, followed by his last name; underneath he inscribed "77," to indicate the year 1877. I was nine at the time.

Indeed it soon began to rain, and I had to retreat inside. The summer storm that followed was strong, but it didn't last long.

Oh yes! I forgot to tell you that the flowers in the picture are geraniums, with a few white petunias as well.

"Camille Daurelle
in the Park
at Yerres"
*1877.*
*Pastel.*

Do you remember this picture? It's the one of Camille you've just seen. You can make your own version of this image with your own crayons or paints. If you decide to use the same colors as in the original, you'll be doing what copyists do when they match their colors with those used by the artist whose work they are trying to imitate. But you are free to make your own choices. Notice the various kinds of strokes Caillebotte employed to produce the look and feel of different things in his picture: short and patchy for the flowers, smooth for the path, many thin lines for Camille's smock, and so forth. You'll have fun trying out various ways you can apply the material you're working with here.

# It's raining! What shall we do?

This is the moment to take out the leaves and flowers you dried and then put into your book.

Go back to pages 18-26.

## Dried flowers and leaves

can be used to decorate all kinds of things, for example the boxes or containers that food comes in. Remove any paper around the container you've selected and then—if you wish—paint the outside any color you like. It is ready now to be decorated with a few of the things you dried. You can attach them with little dabs of paste or glue.

You can also decorate candles with your dried leaves and flowers. It's very simple; just look at the picture to the left. Flatten a candle a bit on one side so it doesn't roll. Warm up an iron slightly (make sure you ask an adult to help you with the iron). Place the flowers on the candle and press on them gently with the iron for a few seconds. When you remove the iron, the flowers will be stuck to the candle, for the warmth of the iron will have softened the wax. The result can be very pretty.

## Make your own stationery

Take a blank sheet of paper and glue some dried leaves to the top. You can arrange them in interesting patterns or shapes. To suggest the shape of a rabbit, for example, you can use a round leaf for the body, two rose petals for the head and one paw, and two thin leaves for the ears. Just stick them down with dots of glue. You can imagine all sorts of other shapes and designs. It's up to you!

"Portrait of Zoé
Caillebotte"
*1877.*
*Oil on canvas.*

Doubtless it was on a rainy day that the painter represented his young cousin Zoé Caillebotte sitting in the corner of a room in which she'd taken shelter.

A fireplace is on the right. Zoé liked this little room, where she came to see Madame Boissière, who would sew there. Sometimes she told stories or taught us songs while she worked. I liked to visit with her, especially when Zoé got her to answer lots of questions.

In this picture, Zoé is wearing an apron to protect her dress from soiling. The room is very bright, for it's lit by a window and two French doors opening onto the garden. What's more, the walls and furniture are covered with a beautiful material decorated with flowers.

# Word game

Twenty-six words having to do with gardens are spelled out below. Can you find them? When you do, color them in like the word "summer" so you won't forget where they are.

| S | M | I | T | C | O | L | O | R |
|---|---|---|---|---|---|---|---|---|
| T | E | R | R | A | R | I | U | M |
| E | H | O | E | I | I | C | J | A |
| M | O | W | E | L | N | H | A | G |
| E | A | E | A | L | D | E | R | P |
| A | K | E | F | E | R | N | S | I |
| L | A | D | Y | B | U | G | L | E |
| P | O | T | P | O | U | R | R | I |
| E | C | R | L | T | R | O | O | T |
| A | Q | I | U | T | L | W | S | U |
| S | U | M | M | E | R | Y | E | W |

76

# Let's make paper flowers

But that must be difficult!

Not at all.

It's as easy as pie, and the results are really beautiful. If you make several flowers, you'll have a bouquet that will last a long time.

Why not make pink daisies?

You'll need pieces of white, yellow, and green construction paper, a pink crayon, cotton, thread, thin metal wire, and a pair of scissors.

Follow the instructions closely.

To make the center of the flower, cut a square with two-inch sides out of the yellow paper. Make a depression in the center so it will hold a small ball of cotton (about as large as green pea) and then sew the cotton ball to the paper square with thread.

To make the petals, cut out a band of the white paper

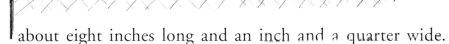

about eight inches long and an inch and a quarter wide.

Color a narrow strip along one of its long sides pink. Don't worry about coloring it all the same: pink flowers are not all precisely the same shade.

Then make make a fringe by cutting all along the same side, but only as far in as you've colored.

Wrap this fringed band around the center and attach the two pieces with the wire. But don't cut the wire; turn the end down to serve as the stem.

Wrap the wire stem in the green paper.

If you want to add leaves, just cut some out of green construction paper, put daubs of glue on one end of each, and attach them to the stem. *Voilà!*

## "Let's hide behind the orange trees"

During the summer, orange trees in big, wooden boxes were kept outside the house at Yerres; they came in handy when Zoé and I played hide-and-seek. In the winter, they were kept in the greenhouse, for they can't stand cold weather. But when they're out, they create a kind of outdoor garden room near the house; they provide both shade and a sense of intimacy. And when they're in bloom, you can smell their rich perfume everywhere, even inside. They provide a wonderful spot to spend a relaxing summer afternoon—reading, talking, or sewing.

Gustave Caillebotte here depicted his brother Martial from the back; he's absorbed in reading a book or newspaper, but maybe he's studying a musical score, for he loved music. Zoé is fascinated by something she's seen in one of the orange crates, perhaps some insects.

The dog, lying in the sun at the edge of the path in the background, seems the happiest of all!

The gracious metal garden furniture, with its delicately curved shapes, is typical of the period. A bed of geraniums is visible in the sunny background, and so is a bit of woods in the upper right corner. It is relaxing just to look at this wonderful garden scene.

"The Orange Trees"
*1878.*
*Oil on canvas.*

# What can one do with oranges?

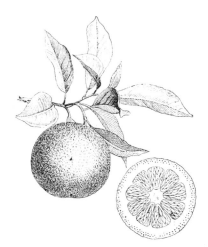

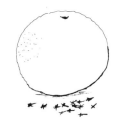

## Cloved oranges

In Caillebotte's time, oranges were rare even if you owned an orange tree, because the season in which they grew was relatively short. Because oranges were so prized, they were often presented as gifts. Cloved oranges were first made in the sixteenth century. Take a firm orange and stick cloves all over it, arranged in rows. It will then give off a delicious perfume. Place it in a closet, a drawer, or wherever you think appropriate.

## Orange candles

*Look at the illustration carefully*

*base of the wick*

*Be sure to keep the wick!*

*a little oil*

Cut a large orange in half and carefully scoop out the pulp, being sure not to tear off the little "wick" inside at the bottom. Dry this wick very carefully with a paper towel. Then pour a little oil around it. Meanwhile, cut some shapes—stars, circles, half-moons—into the other half of the orange skin. Ask your parents or another adult to light the wick, and then you can place the two halves together. The result? A charming lamp, ideal for when you eat supper outside in the summer.

"Portrait of
Camille Daurelle"
*1877.*
*Pastel.*

Here's a portrait of me. Caillebotte had me pose for it in the garden. I had to keep still so he could capture the expression on my face. That was no fun! It's a good thing everyone has cameras today.

The lawn and part of a path are visible behind me. My face is in a blue shadow and my clothes are dark, which makes me stand out against the light background colors.

The painter liked this portrait; he decided to exhibit it in an art show in Paris in 1880. When I look at it now, I regret not having gone to the exhibition: it would have been fun to hide like a mouse nearby and listen to what people said about it!

# My vacation diary

Illustrated by photographs:
- my successes as a gardener
- the most beautiful sunsets I saw
- the recipes I made
- the walks I took
- me fishing
- my friends

And my favorite memory

# June

# July

# August

## "Farewell"

This picture is full of memories for me.

It reminds me of the many beautiful days spent at Yerres in the grand, Italian-style, white house; of walks through the garden; of moments in the woods or by the river.

The building in the left background is the dairy, which we called the mountain house because it resembles wooden buildings in the mountains. It also has a wooden balcony.

In the middle of this painting, you can see two flower beds that Gustave Caillebotte liked to paint.

This picture sums up my life at Yerres, so I've decided to use it to say good-bye.

"The Garden
at Yerres"
c. *1876.*
*Oil on canvas.*

# THAT'S A POSSIBILITY!

## A Book About What Might Happen

## BRUCE GOLDSTONE

Henry Holt and Company

NEW YORK

# What's a Possibility?

**If something can happen, it's a possibility.**

Will this mouse find the cheese?

## That's a possibility!

If one of these balloons **POPS**, will it be the monkey?

# That's a possibility!

What are some other **possibilities?**

3

# That's Impossible!

Something that can't happen is impossible.

Might this ball knock down 10 pins? Sure—that's called a strike.

Might this ball knock down 4 pins? What about no pins at all? Those are possibilities, too. But could this ball knock down 12 pins in one roll? Nope, that's **impossible!** Can you see why?

There are only 10 pins in a bowling lane—so you can't knock down 12 pins at once.

4

Will a **chicken** hatch from this egg?

That's a possibility!

Will a **snake** hatch from this egg?

That's a possibility!

Will a **spider** hatch from this egg?

That's a possibility!

Will an **elephant** hatch from this egg?

That's impossible!

Some animals hatch from eggs and some don't.
Elephants don't, so unless you're reading a made-up story,
it's **impossible** for an elephant to hatch from an egg.

5

# That's for Certain

If something is sure to happen, it is certain.

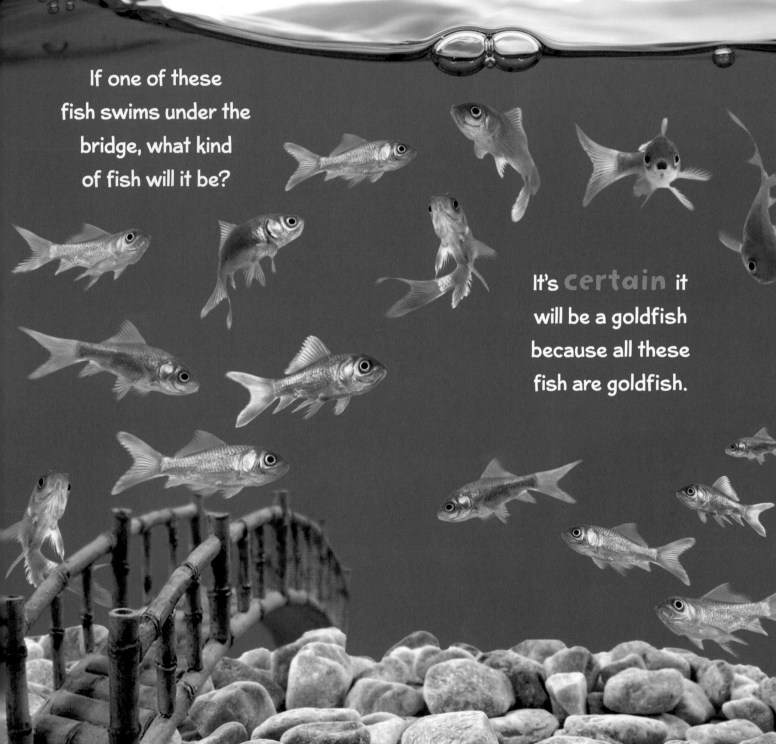

If one of these fish swims under the bridge, what kind of fish will it be?

It's **certain** it will be a goldfish because all these fish are goldfish.

If someone cuts these strings, what is **certain** to happen to the puppet?

# Will It BEE Likely?

Some possible things are more likely to happen than others.

Will this bee land
on a white flower?

That's possible, but it
isn't very **likely**.

If something is more likely to happen than something else, it's **probable**.
Will this butterfly land on one of the purple flowers?
That's **probable**. Can you see why?

# Possibilities on the Wing

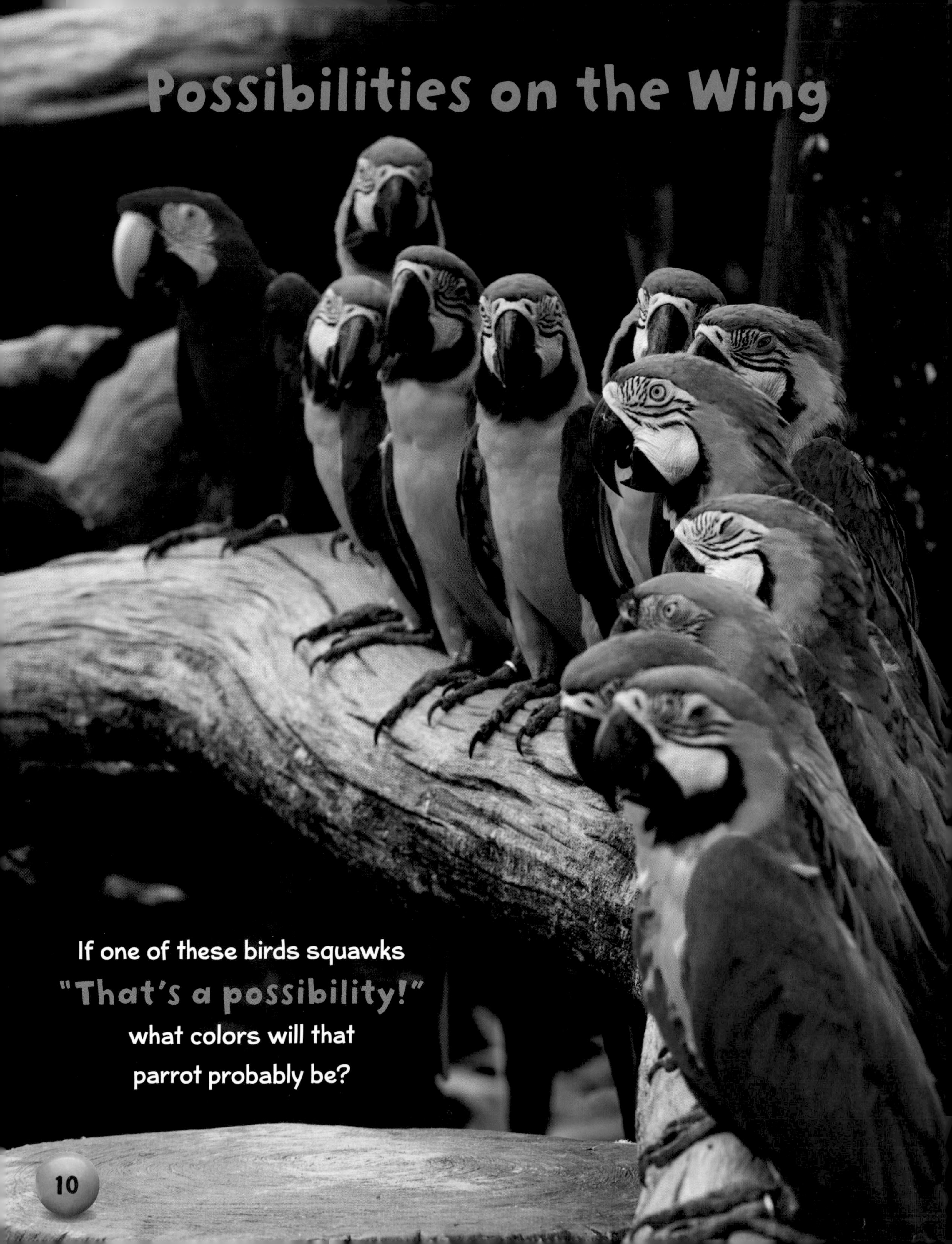

If one of these birds squawks
**"That's a possibility!"**
what colors will that
parrot probably be?

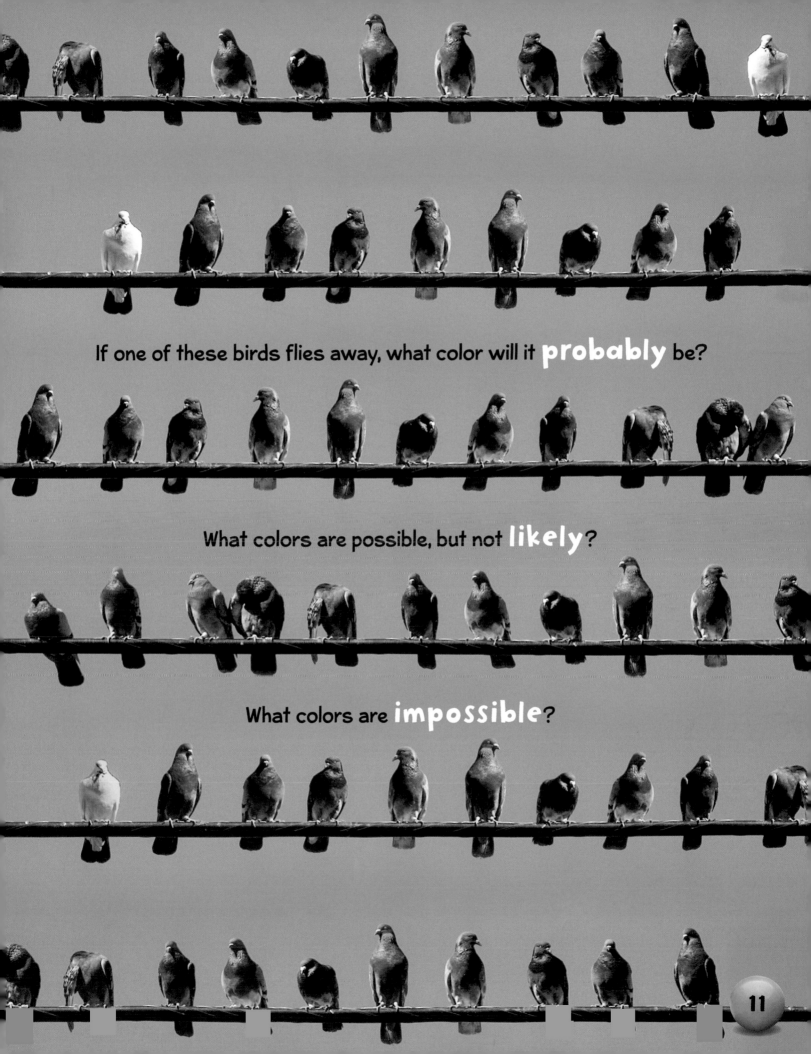

If one of these birds flies away, what color will it **probably** be?

What colors are possible, but not **likely**?

What colors are **impossible**?

# A Chance for Change

If something is possible but not likely to happen, it is improbable.

These gumballs are in this machine.

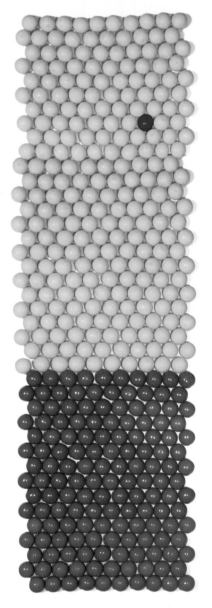

What color gumball will
you probably get?
What other colors are possible?
Is it possible to get a red
gumball? Sure, it's possible—
but it's **improbable**.

These prizes are in this machine.

**200** rings

**100** mini erasers

**50** lizards

**25** plastic bugs

**1** compass

What prize are you most likely to get? What other prizes are **probable**? Which prize is **improbable**?

# Pet Possibilities

If this cat pounces on one ball of yarn, what color will it probably be?

What other color is **possible**?

Can you think of a color
that's **impossible**
for this cat to get?

Suppose this dog eats just one of these biscuits.
(Okay, how likely is that?)

What shape biscuit will
he **probably** chomp?

What other shapes
are **possible**?

What shapes are
**impossible**?

15

# That Seems Likely

Your imagination can help you think of possibilities, too.

What will **probably** happen when this jumper hits the water?

What will this ant **probably** do with the leaf?
It might eat the leaf. That's a good possibility.

It might carry the leaf to its nest.
That's a **possibility**, too.

Will the ant cut the leaf
into little pieces and
throw it around
like confetti at a
surprise party?
That's not possible
in real life—it's
only a possibility
in a story.

# Odds Aren't Strange

The chances that something will happen are called odds.

When you flip a coin, there are 2 possibilities: it can land **heads** or tails.

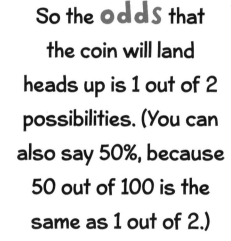

So the **odds** that the coin will land heads up is 1 out of 2 possibilities. (You can also say 50%, because 50 out of 100 is the same as 1 out of 2.)

Every time you toss a coin, the odds are the same. It doesn't matter what happened before you tossed the coin.

Suppose you toss a coin **5** times and it lands tails up all five times.

What are the chances it will land tails up on the **6**th toss?

You might be tempted to say that the coin should land heads, because it's been tails so many times.

But the odds don't change. There's still a 1 in 2 chance that the coin will land tails up.

Suppose you toss a coin and it lands heads up **10** times in a row.

What are the odds it will land heads up on the **11**th toss?

# Spin to Win

Many games depend on what might happen. Some games use spinners.

If you spin this spinner, what color will the pointer **probably** land on? Why?

If you spin this spinner, what color will you **probably** get? Why?

20

The goal of this game is to get to the finish first.
You can choose which spinner to spin. Then you move
the number of spaces the pointer lands on.

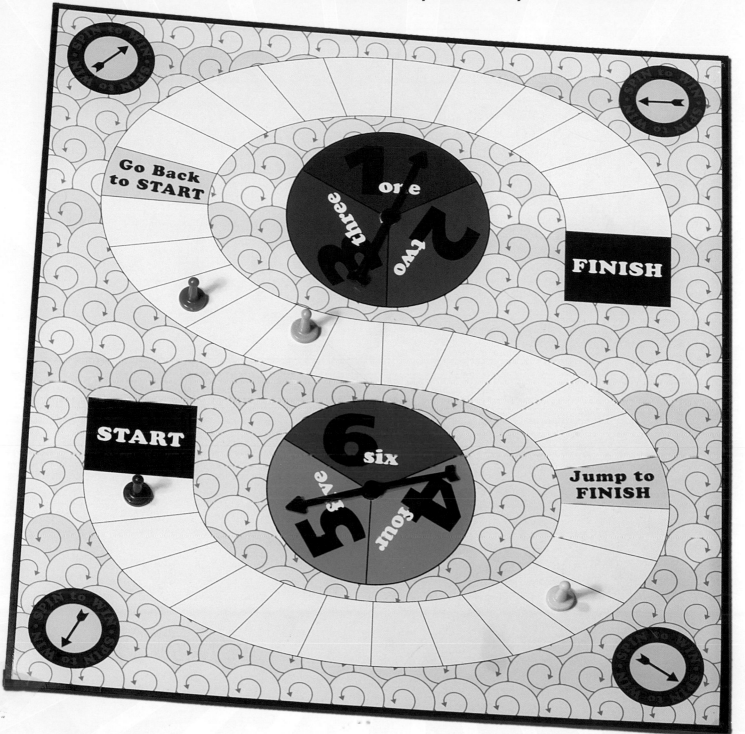

What numbers are **possible**? Which spinner do you think
the red player should use? What about the other players?

# It's in the Cards

A deck of cards has a lot of possibilities.

Every deck has 52 cards (and sometimes a joker or two).

What are the chances this card is a red card?

Remember that half of the cards in a deck are red. So there's a 50% chance this card is red. (What's the other **possibility**?)

Is this card **probably** a king? Is it **possibly** a king?

Can this card be a 17 of clubs?

Is this card **probably** greater than 3? Why?

Is it likely that this card is a diamond? Is it **possible**?

# On a Roll

If you roll one die, what are the possibilities?

Can you roll an even number?

## That's a possibility!

You might roll 2, 4, or 6.

You will **probably** roll a number greater than 2. Can you see why?

It's **impossible** to roll a zero. What are some other impossible rolls?

24

**2** **3** **4** **5** **6** **7** **8** **9** **10** **11** **12**

What if you roll two dice?
This chart shows all the possible
sums—and the possible ways
you can roll each of them.

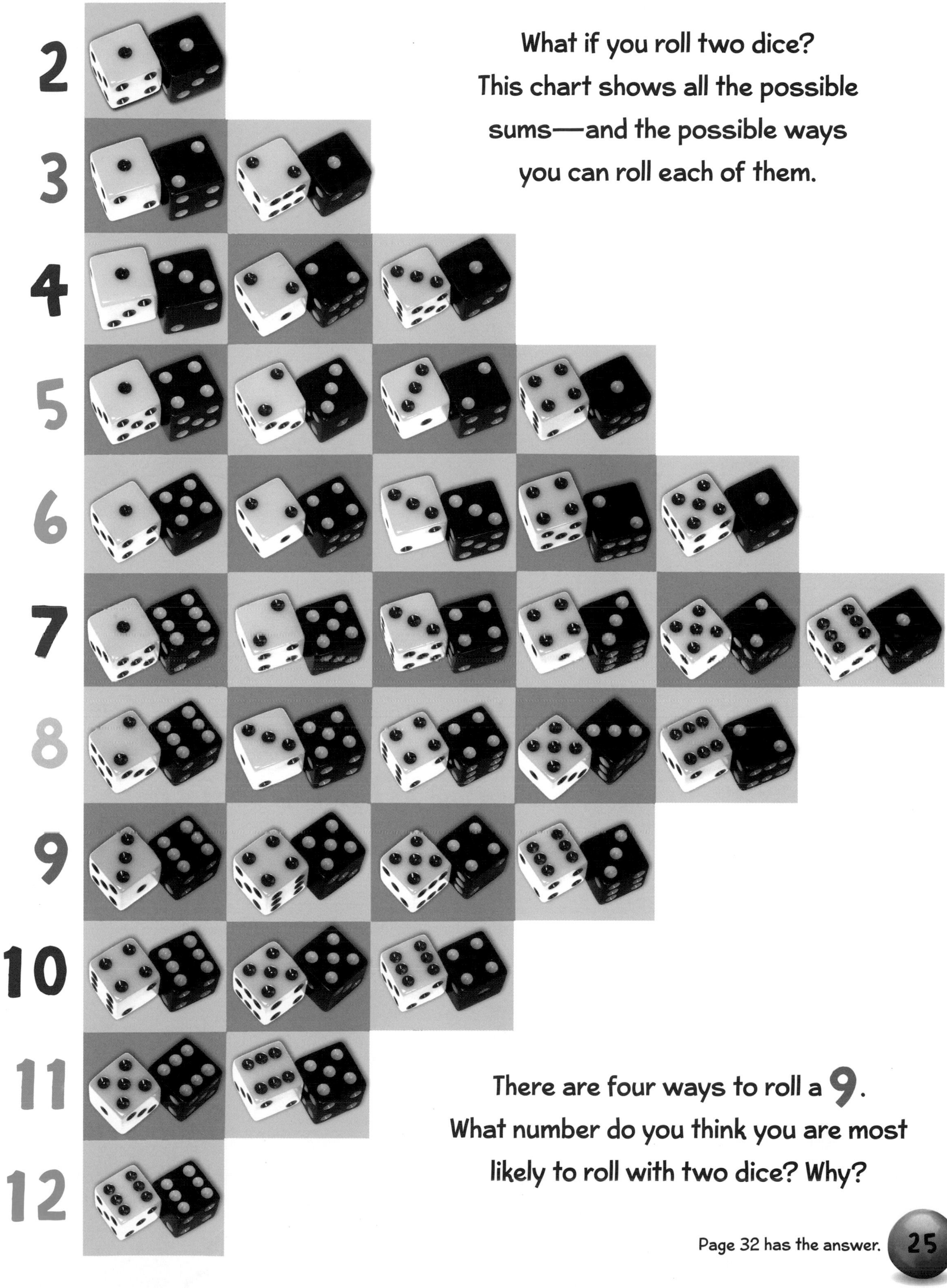

There are four ways to roll a **9**.
What number do you think you are most
likely to roll with two dice? Why?

Page 32 has the answer.

# BEARLY Possible

This is Squidgy the Bear.

He has **10** shirts and **10** pairs of pants.

How many different outfits can Squidgy wear?
You can make a list to show possible combinations.

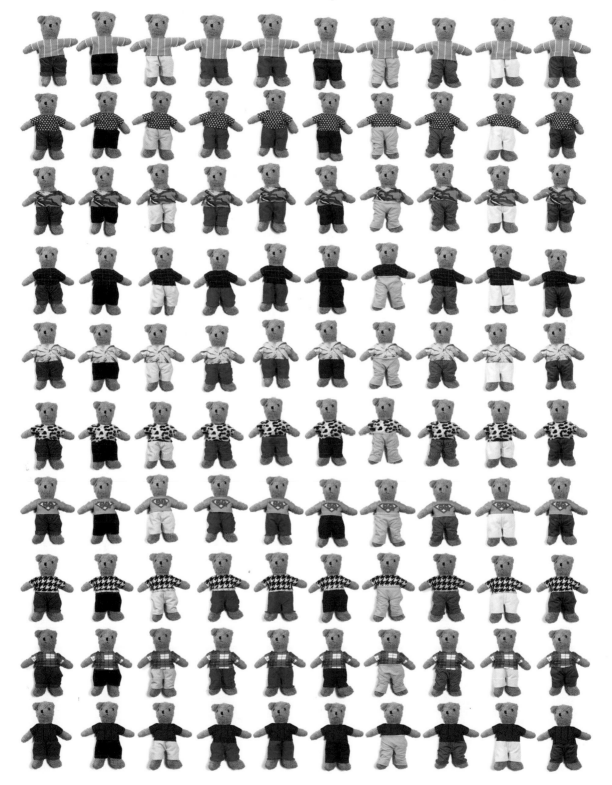

If Squidgy wears a different outfit each day, might he wear a leopard-print
shirt and purple pants tomorrow? That's **bearly** possible—
he has a 1 in 100 chance of wearing that outfit.

# Race Results

If a rabbit and a frog (let's call him Ribbit) have a race, who could win?

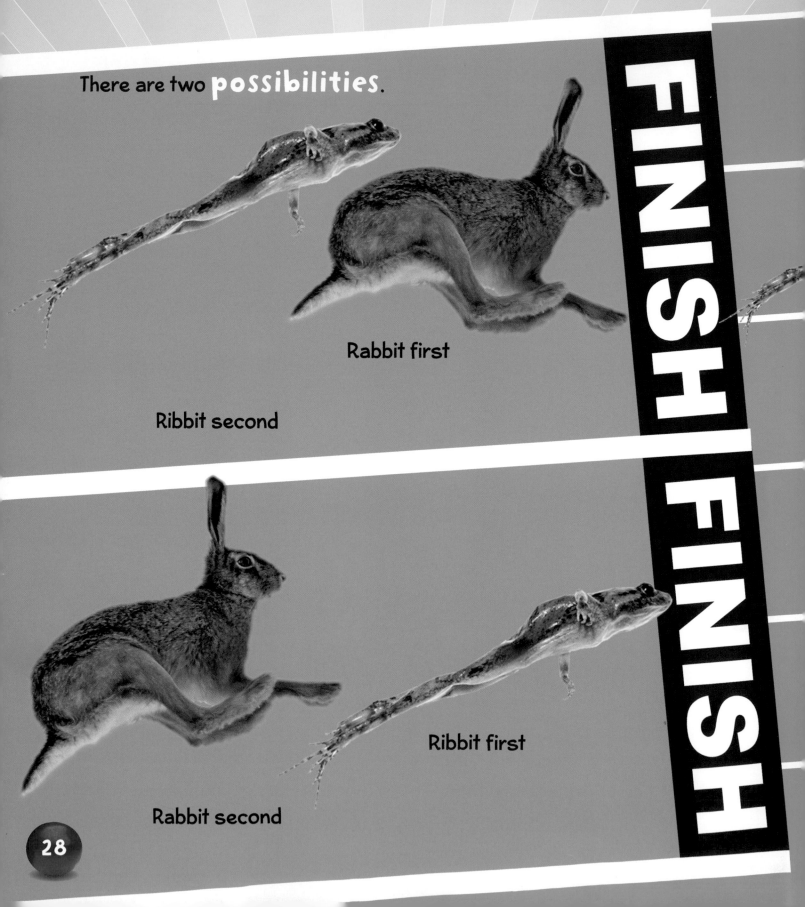

There are two **possibilities**.

Rabbit first

Ribbit second

Ribbit first

Rabbit second

FINISH FINISH

28

What if Robot joins the race?

How many **possibilities** are there when these three runners have a race?

Can you say all the possibilities together without getting your tongue twisted?

That's a **possibility,** but is it **probable**?

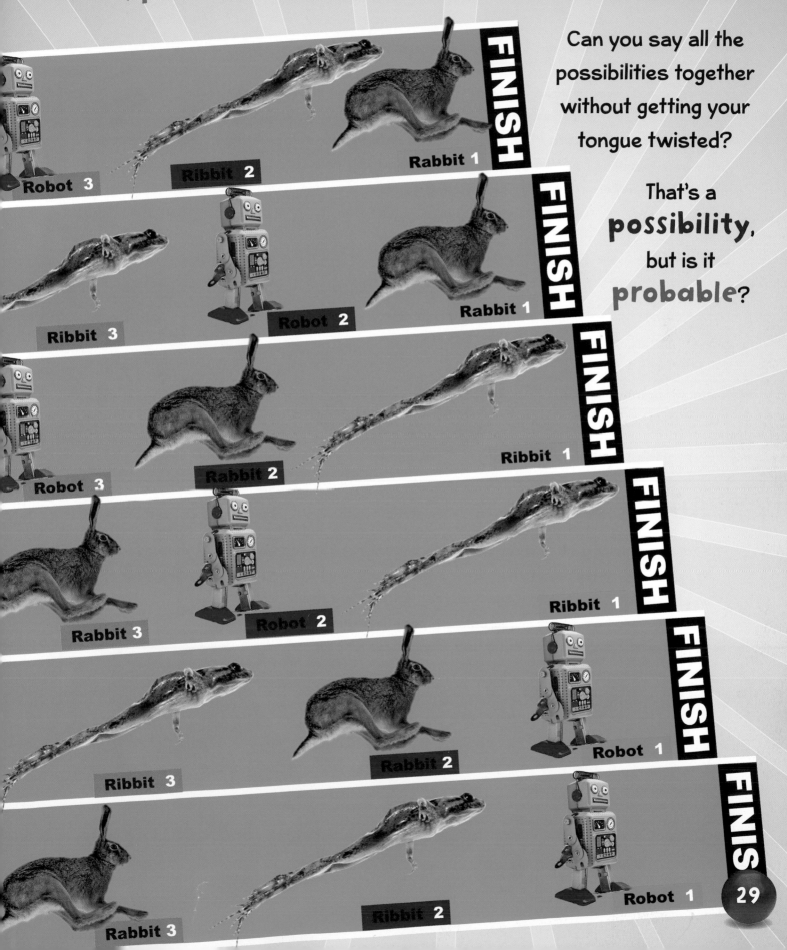

# Try This at Home

## Paper Plate Spinner

Here's an easy way to make a spinner. Start with two paper plates. Fold one in half to make a ruler. Place the folded plate on top of the other plate and follow the straight edge with a marker. Then turn the folded plate and repeat to create sections (you can create any even number of sections). Then take one paper clip, open it to form an L, and poke the point through the center of the plate. Place another paper clip over the upright part of the first paper clip. Flick the paper clip with your finger and see where it lands.

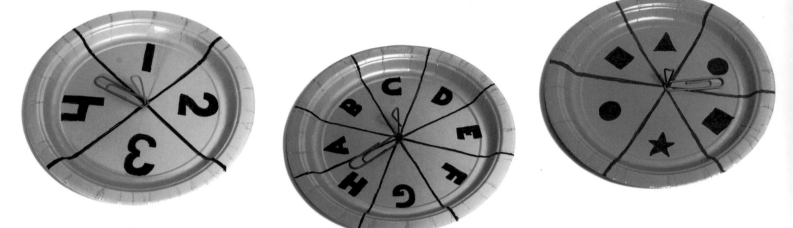

## Guess Again

Here's a guessing game that can be as easy or challenging as you want. Begin by asking someone to hide two or three objects that are the same shape in a bag or a sock. You might use marbles, plastic blocks, or paper clips. When you reach into the bag, feel to see how many objects are inside, but don't peek. Take one out, look at what color it is, then put it back. Repeat this step as many times as you want until you think you know what color the hidden objects are. Write down your guess, then empty the bag to check. Were you right? The game gets more challenging when there are more objects hidden inside. You might keep a tally of your picks to help you think about what's probably inside.

# A Few More Thoughts on What's Possible

**Probability** is the math word for how likely something is to take place. But we talk about **possibility** all the time, not just in math class. Whenever we think about what might happen, that's a possibility. What will the weather be like tomorrow? Will it rain? If it does, might I get hit by lightning?

We often use numbers to talk about odds or chances. The numbers help describe how likely something is. Still worried about that lightning? Well, experts say that your chances of getting struck by lightning this year are about 1 in a million. That doesn't sound so bad. But if you make it through this year without getting hit, does that mean you'll be more likely to get struck next year? Nope. The two years are independent—just like tossing a coin. No matter how many times a coin lands heads up, the odds that it will land tails up on the next toss remain the same.

Of course, words help us talk about probability, too. This book presents many of them—*possible, impossible, certain, likely, unlikely, odds, chances*. Here are a few more words that mathematicians use to talk about probability:

**Outcomes.** Something that happens is an outcome. A possible outcome is something that might happen. Outcomes that involve more than one thing can be combinations or permutations.

**Combinations.** Order doesn't make any difference in a combination. For example, Squidgy's 100 outfits (page 27) are combinations. It doesn't matter if he puts on the shirt or pants first. He still ends up with 100 outfits.

**Permutations.** Order makes a big difference in a permutation. Races, like the battle between Ribbit, Rabbit, and Robot (page 29), are examples of permutations. Order makes the difference between winning and losing. When there are three runners, there are six possible permutations. Another example of permutations is the numbers you use to open a lock. I know, we call them combination locks. But we should really call them permutation locks. If you don't dial the numbers in the right order, the lock won't open.

Probability can help you predict what will happen. Will you win a big lottery jackpot? That's a possibility, but not a big one. (The odds are different depending on your state, but they're usually about 18 million to 1.) But whenever you want to talk about what might happen, the language of possibility will make your discussion more accurate and more interesting. That's more than a possibility. It's a sure thing.

## HAPPY POSSIBILITIES!

Bruce Goldstone

# Notes

## Page 21

Most of the time, players should choose the 4-5-6 spinner. They'll get a higher number and move faster than if they use the 1-2-3 spinner. The red and green players should choose the 4-5-6 spinner. But there are two cases where this is a bad idea: when you want to land on one space and when you want to avoid one space. The yellow player wants to land on "Jump to FINISH." The blue player doesn't want to land on "Go Back to START." They're both better off choosing the 1-2-3 spinner.

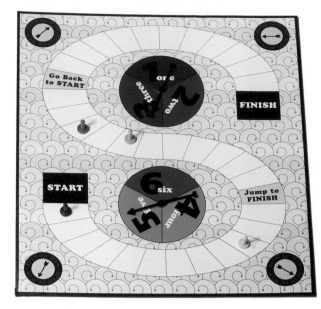

## Page 25

You are most likely to roll a 7 with two dice. There are six ways to roll a 7—that's more than for any other number.

Thanks to Kan Nagata for his expert quarter-tossing and John Sabatini for his expert eye.

Henry Holt and Company, LLC, *Publishers since 1866*
175 Fifth Avenue, New York, New York 10010
mackids.com

Henry Holt® is a registered trademark of Henry Holt and Company, LLC.
Copyright © 2013 by Bruce Goldstone
All rights reserved.

Library of Congress Cataloging-in-Publication Data
Goldstone, Bruce.
That's a possibility! : a book about what might happen / Bruce Goldstone. — First edition.
    pages   cm
Summary: "With colorful photographs and interactive examples, Bruce Goldstone introduces children to the ideas of something being possible, probable, or impossible. Each spread features an easy-to-understand, fun scenario such as dice rolling and bowling, with questions about probable outcomes and simple explanations. In the vein of GREAT ESTIMATIONS, this is a perfect book for getting across important math concepts in a fun way." — Provided by publisher
Audience: 7–10.
ISBN 978-0-8050-8998-1 (hardback)
1. Probabilities—Juvenile literature.  I. Title.
QA273.16.G65 2013   519.2—dc23   2012036691

Henry Holt books may be purchased for business or promotional use. For information on bulk purchases please contact Macmillan Corporate and Premium Sales Department at (800) 221-7945 x5442 or by e-mail at specialmarkets@macmillan.com.

First Edition—2013 / Designed by April Ward
Printed in China by Macmillan Production Asia Ltd., Kowloon Bay, Hong Kong (vendor code: 10)

1 3 5 7 9 10 8 6 4 2

For Squidgy,
the best-traveled
and best-dressed
bear I know
—B. G.